# About the a

**Chris Hudson** is an experienced t
dedicated to promoting high-qua
in primary schools. He provides regular INSET for
on a variety of themes related to the Bible and Christianity, together with Barnabas RE Day storytelling, drama and
music workshops for schoolchildren.

**Jane Butcher** trained and worked as a teacher, moving into
church ministry in 1993. She has led training sessions and
seminars in a variety of schools, churches and dioceses on
different aspects of RE and children's ministry, and is an
accredited Godly Play teacher. She is responsible for developing BRF's Faith in Homes ministry.

**Joy Howell** joined the Barnabas in Schools freelance team
in 2011, leading RE Days, and is part of the team writing
materials for new RE Days and INSET. Joy also works in her
own church, other churches and local schools, focusing on
children's and youth work. Before this, Joy trained for and
worked in primary education for 16 years.

**Ken Wylie** has always enjoyed sport and, through it, fully
understands that winning isn't everything. From a background in mime, he has worked in schools engaging children
with creative storytelling for over 15 years. He is currently
training to become an Anglican priest.

All four authors are or have been part of BRF's Barnabas
in Schools team. For further details about our Barnabas RE
Days and INSET, see page 92.

Text copyright © Chris Hudson 2011
Additional text copyright © Jane Butcher, Joy Howell and Ken Wylie 2015
Illustrations copyright © Simon Smith 2011
The authors assert the moral right to be identified as the authors of this work

**Published by**
**The Bible Reading Fellowship**
15 The Chambers, Vineyard
Abingdon OX14 3FE
United Kingdom
Tel: +44 (0)1865 319700
Email: enquiries@brf.org.uk
Website: www.brf.org.uk
BRF is a Registered Charity

ISBN 978 1 84101 742 6

**First published 2011 as** *Who Comes First?*
**Revised edition published 2015**

10 9 8 7 6 5 4 3 2 1 0

**Acknowledgements**
Unless otherwise stated, scripture quotations are taken from the Contemporary English
Version of the Bible published by HarperCollins Publishers, copyright © 1991, 1992,
1995 American Bible Society.

Scriptures quoted from the Good News Bible published by The Bible Societies/Harper-
Collins Publishers Ltd, UK © American Bible Society 1966, 1971, 1976, 1992, used with
permission.

Scripture taken from the New Century Version®. Copyright © 2005 by Thomas Nelson,
Inc. Used by permission. All rights reserved.

Cover photos: top photo © JJ pixs/ Shutterstock.com; bottom photo © Monkey Business
Images/Shutterstock.com

Every effort has been made to trace and contact copyright owners for material used
in this resource. We apologise for any inadvertent omissions or errors, and would ask
those concerned to contact us so that full acknowledgement can be made in the future.

A catalogue record for this book is available from the British Library

Printed and bound by CPI Group (UK) Ltd, Croydon CR0 4YY

# What Makes a Winner?

Chris Hudson, Jane Butcher,
Joy Howell and Ken Wylie

A cross-curricular classroom and Collective Worship
resource on learning life lessons from sport

— Acknowledgements —

*With special thanks to Lilo Ljubisic, Haile Gebrselassie
and Jos Hermens for their help and advice.*

# Contents

## Stories and lesson plans

Key themes: Dependence, Racism, Segregation, Overcoming difficulties

Key themes: Dependence, Friendship, Equality, Loving enemies, World War II

Key themes: Discipline, Poverty, Prayer, Aspirations

Key themes: Discipline, Principles, Inspiration, Adaptability

Key themes: Determination, Dedication, Disability, Equality, Inequality

## Material for assemblies and Collective Worship

*

# Introduction

Does sport have anything of value to teach us?

Think about the Olympic and Paralympic Games, which aim to celebrate Respect, Excellence, Friendship, Courage, Determination, Inspiration and Equality. Indeed, Pierre de Coubertin (founder of the 'revived' modern Games) believed they would foster world peace:

*May joy and good fellowship reign, and in this manner, may the Olympic Torch pursue its way through ages, increasing friendly understanding among nations, for the good of a humanity always more enthusiastic, more courageous and more pure.*

Was he being slightly naive? The ancient Greek Games could be ultra-violent and highly nationalistic. Events such as the Pankration (a form of extreme wrestling) were brutal and occasionally fatal, and many of the events were simply the display of battlefield skills under competition rules. Wars weren't necessarily cancelled during Olympic years as they were meant to be, women and slaves were banned from competing, some teams were refused entry, and many Greek cities used the event to intimidate their rivals. In more recent times, the modern Games have witnessed terrorism (Munich 1972), extreme nationalism (Berlin 1936 and others), the settling of 'old scores' (the 1956 Russia/Hungary water polo final), political protests or boycotts (Moscow 1980 and many others) and the use of illegal performance-enhancing drugs and other treatments by a number of athletes from a range of nationalities.

And yet... there is still something marvellous when we see a well-won victory by a skilled athlete working at the peak of their fitness. Sporting competitions can promote so many positive messages about discipline, dedication and determination. There are rules to follow, team members to encourage, and supporters to lift your spirits and cheer you on.

This resource is intended to help you to use sporting endeavour as a means of exploring key values with your pupils in Religious Education, PSHE, Citizenship and Literacy lessons, assemblies and Collective Worship. Think back to your own schooldays and the way sport was used to reinforce school values. My own admittedly rather negative experiences from school sports suggest that PE can sometimes be part of an unconscious 'hidden curriculum', celebrating values that talk about certain sorts of people being intrinsically 'better' than others.

*What Makes a Winner?* aims to counter that agenda by encouraging children to ask hard questions about 'sporting values', to respond to true-life stories in a variety of ways, and to reflect positively on what it all has to do with them.

*

# How to use this book

The suggested lesson material will need to be adapted by you to suit the different aptitudes and abilities in your class. There is a mix of suggested activities to accompany each story, but, in RE lessons, always try to relate the activities to your RE objectives, which means including *at least* one of the suggested RE activities in the lesson.

Of course, a cross-curricular approach will allow you to tick a lot of other subject 'boxes' and to approach the same topic from a variety of angles with a variety of approaches— but please don't sacrifice the RE.

This book approaches the topic from a broadly Christian perspective, but others will have insights too. Hopefully, the lesson material will get your class talking about their own values and generate discussion across different faiths and beliefs; as the class teacher, you may want to add stories and ideas from other traditions, using the model presented here. The key message is probably... Enjoy!

The suggested websites are useful resources but they can be subject to change, so you should always check the current state of a website for suitability before sending children towards it for research purposes.

# Stories and lesson plans

# Wilma Rudolph

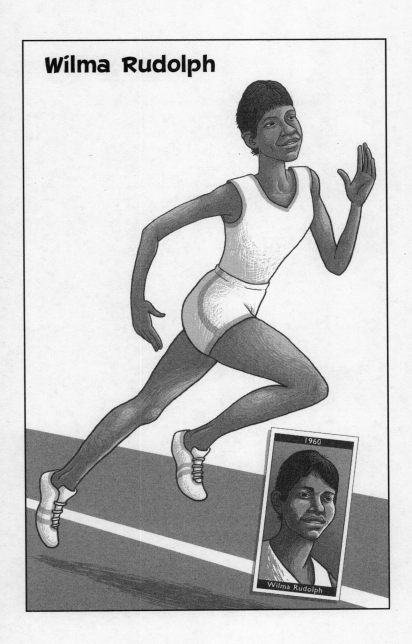

1960

Wilma Rudolph

# Wilma Rudolph

*Sprinter, 100 metres and 200 metres*
*Competed in Rome, 1960*

## Key themes

Dependence, Racism, Segregation,
Overcoming difficulties

## Key quote

*The triumph can't be had without the struggle.*
*And I know what struggle is. I have spent a lifetime*
*trying to share what it has meant to be a woman*
*first in the world of sports, so that other young*
*women have a chance to reach their dreams.*
WILMA RUDOLPH

---

# Introduction

Ask pupils to discuss in pairs what their proudest moment
has been, and ask a few to share this with the class.

## Story retelling

As a child, Wilma was always getting sick. Although
there was never enough money, she always felt loved

and cared for. However, her family couldn't afford a doctor.

So when Wilma contracted polio (a disease that wastes away your leg muscles), the only doctor in town who would treat her said she would never walk again. Wilma's mother didn't agree. There was a university hospital 50 miles away that she knew would treat her child—so twice a week, for two years, Wilma was taken there for physiotherapy. She had to walk with a crutch and wear a metal brace on one leg and corrective shoes on both feet just to walk straight. Her family were taught how to exercise Wilma at home as well, and they did it, brothers and sisters too. So, by the age of twelve, Wilma didn't need that kind of help any more. She had recovered. And now she wanted to run.

At high school, she made the basketball team and also practised hard at a local running track. After being spotted by a local coach, she was soon competing and winning at the state athletic championships. By 1956, she was part of the USA's team in the 4 x 100 metre relay, and took home a bronze medal for it— and the 1960 Rome Games saw her take three gold medals for the 100 metres, 200 metres and 4 x 100 metre relay. She was now breaking athletic records set by men, and going further.

Wilma then represented her country at other athletics meetings around the world—and kept on winning in competition after competition. All of a sudden she was famous! The US president invited her to see him at the White House, and there were further parades to join and awards to win as she travelled the world. It was all very new and exciting for a young woman.

But then, one day, an invitation to a special event made her stop and think very hard. Wilma's own childhood town of Clarksville had invited her back for a civic reception to celebrate her achievements. There would be music, speeches and thousands of people attending. But it would be 'segregated', as everything was in Clarksville. At that time, parts of the USA practised 'segregation', where people of different races were kept apart as much as possible. Segregation meant that Wilma had to ride at the back of the bus, could only go to school with other black children and was only ever seen by a black doctor. And the civic reception to celebrate her gold medal performances would be segregated too. Wilma thought very hard; then she put her foot down—and said 'No.' What? No.

She *wouldn't* come to a civic reception in her home town that was segregated. If the races couldn't mix freely there, then she wouldn't go. It was a powerful decision. The city council had to think very hard too, but they couldn't ignore her. So finally they gave in. The big day came—and 40,000 local people of all races and backgrounds turned up to cheer their sporting heroine, together. It was a brilliant moment, and afterwards Wilma said it was one of the best things she ever did.

# Key points from the story

- Wilma, with her family, had to work hard to overcome her childhood polio, because black people then usually had a much lower income, and they were not allowed to use the same doctors and hospitals in Clarksville as white people.
- 'Segregation' is not legal now in the USA because of a strong campaign led by Dr Martin Luther King and other people like Wilma Rudolph.
- Their campaign was peaceful and non-violent, based on the teachings of Mohandas Gandhi and the biblical life and words of Jesus of Nazareth.
- Wilma was a devout Baptist Christian whose faith expressed itself in a desire for racial justice, in the same way that it later led her to support the work of evangelists such as Dr Billy Graham.

# Activities

## Religious Education: Key Stage 1

Wilma used her skills and talents to make a difference. We are all good at something. How do we use what we are good at? Jesus once said to his friends:

*You are like light for the whole world. A city built on top of a hill cannot be hidden, and no one would light a lamp and put it under a clay pot. A lamp is placed on a lampstand, where it can give light to*

*everyone in the house. Make your light shine, so that others will see the good that you do and will praise your Father in heaven.*
MATTHEW 5:14–16

- Ask pupils to stand and mime something they are good at. Take time to ask them about what they have chosen. Ask pupils to mime something they can do that would help someone else. Take time to ask them about what they have chosen.
- Give each child a picture of a candle with light rays coming from the flame. On the rays, they should write or draw the things they are good at that would make the world a 'brighter', kinder or fairer place.

# Religious Education: Key Stage 2

- Segregation in the USA was finally defeated after a long campaign by African-American churches like the one Wilma attended. Read the following Bible passages. Which of these do you think would have most influenced Wilma to take a stand against segregation? Using a five-part diamond grid, put the letter of the most important at the top, the next three in the middle, and the least important at the bottom. Explain your choices.

A   'I give you peace, the kind of peace that only I can give. It isn't like the peace that this world can give. So don't be worried or afraid' (John 14:27).
B   'If you have faith when you pray, you will be given whatever you ask for' (Matthew 21:22).
C   'Faith in Christ Jesus… makes each of you equal with each other, whether you are a Jew or a Greek, a slave or a free person, a man or a woman' (Galatians 3:28).
D   'I tell you not to try to get even with a person who has done something to you' (Matthew 5:39).
E   'We often suffer, but we are never crushed. Even when we don't know what to do, we never give up. In times of trouble, God is with us, and when we are knocked down, we get up again' (2 Corinthians 4:8–9).

To reproduce these quotes, download the pdf file at www.barnabasinschools.org.uk/9781841017426/

- Wilma used her talents and skills to make a difference. If you have talents and skills, what responsibilities do you have to use them? Jesus once said to his followers:

*'You are like light for the whole world. A city built on top of a hill cannot be hidden, and no one would light a lamp and put it under a clay pot. A lamp is placed on a lampstand, where it can give light to everyone in the house. Make your light shine, so that others will see the good that you do and will praise your Father in heaven.'*
MATTHEW 5:14–16

In the middle of a page, draw a candle or an Olympic flame with your name on it. Nearby, show rays of light flying away from it. What skills or talents do you have that could help make the world a 'brighter', kinder and fairer place? Write them or draw them on the rays of light. What would be a good title for this picture?

# PSHE/Citizenship/Literacy

- Wilma demanded respect for herself and others. We can use the word 'respect' to mean all sorts of things. With a partner, try to come up with three sentences that use the word to mean different things. Then try to create a dictionary definition that lists all the possible meanings of the word, and write it out.

    Now consult a printed dictionary and copy out its definition of the word 'respect'. In what ways are your definitions similar and different? What do you think Wilma's story has to say about respect? Draw the five connected rings that make up the Olympic flag, and inside the rings write five words that you think are needed to create a world where everyone shows respect to each other.

- Read these comments from Wilma Rudolph.

    *When I was going through my transition of being famous, I tried to ask God, why was I here? What was my purpose? Surely, it wasn't just to win three gold medals. There has to be more to this life than that.*

*What do you do after you are world famous and 19 or 20 and you have sat with prime ministers, kings and queens, the Pope? Do you go back home and take a job? What do you do to keep your sanity? You come back to the real world.*

*Winning is great, sure, but if you are really going to do something in life, the secret is learning how to lose. Nobody goes undefeated all the time. If you can pick up after a crushing defeat, and go on to win again, you are going to be a champion someday.*

*No matter what accomplishments you make, somebody helps you.*

To reproduce these quotes, download the pdf file at www.barnabasinschools.org.uk/9781841017426/

- Imagine Wilma had just received a letter from a child saying, 'One day I want to be a famous athlete like you.' What do these quotes reveal about Wilma's attitude to becoming a world-famous athlete? What thoughts would she put into her reply? Write the letter.

- Wilma went on to do many other things. Find out the rest of her story at **www.gardenofpraise.com/ibdwilma.htm**. List what you think were her three greatest achievements after winning her gold medals.

# Carl Ludwig 'Luz' Long and Jesse Owens

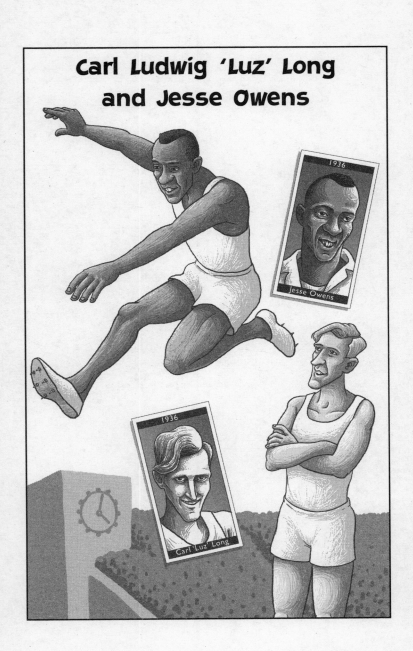

*

# Carl Ludwig 'Luz' Long and Jesse Owens

*Long jump, 100 metres and 200 metres*
*Competed in Berlin, 1936*

### Key themes

Dependence, Friendship, Equality,
Loving enemies, World War II

### Key quote

*Friendships born on the field of athletic strife are the*
*real gold of competition. Awards become corroded,*
*friends gather no dust.*

JESSE OWENS

---

## Introduction

Ask if you can ever be friends with someone against whom
you are competing.

### Story retelling

Something wasn't right, but what? Jesse had made
three jumps to try to qualify for the long jump finals,

and none of them was good enough. The local favourite, Luz Long, was in the final, no question—he was on good form today. But Jesse wasn't, and he knew it. After all his training and getting a place in the United States Olympic team, he wasn't jumping well enough. He only had one jump left. If it wasn't good, he would be out of the finals.

This was Berlin in 1936—Hitler's Summer Games. Adolf Hitler, Chancellor of Germany, had said that this was the time to show how white Aryan Germans could outperform anyone with a darker skin—such as Jesse, who was African-American. But now, with one more chance to qualify for the final, Jesse didn't know what to do. He was about to be called for his last jump, but there was nothing left to give. He was going to fail, and dreaded the thought.

He heard his name again, spoken in a German accent, and felt a warm hand on his shoulder. Was it the official in charge? He looked up. No. It was the German, his enemy, the man he had to beat. But the German was saying something.

'I'm Luz Long. I think I know what's wrong. You're like me. You're giving everything when you jump. But you're afraid of fouling again, aren't you?'

Jesse nodded.

'So you're jumping short,' continued Luz. 'I was doing that last year in the Cologne Games. You just need to take off from further back. That way, you can give everything. Come on. I'll put my towel down to mark the place for you.'

The take-off. Yes, it was so simple, but it needed Jesse's toughest opponent to point it out. What was happening? No matter. Luz marked a jumping-off place six inches back from the jumping board, and stood back to watch as Jesse made his run.

Jesse started slowly with a slow stride, then ran faster, faster, then the take-off... and he felt as if he was flying. He landed. The officials got out their measuring tapes. Over 26 feet! Yes! He was in the finals! But why had it happened like this?

That evening, he met Luz for coffee, and asked him what he thought of Hitler's ideas, the ones about some races of people being better than others. Luz said they were all rubbish. *He* wasn't a Nazi, although he did love his country—and if there was a war, he'd serve in the army to defend Germany and his family. Jesse knew that this was a man who could be a good friend. So over the next few days, they kept meeting to drink coffee and swap stories as Jesse won gold medals for the 100 metres, the 200 metres and the relay.

Then came the day for the long jump final. Towards the end, as the other competitors dropped out, it became clear that the gold would go either to Luz or to Jesse. Luz took his final jump, an amazing effort. He flew through the air, landed—and set a new Olympic record. The German crowd in the stadium cheered their hero. But now it was Jesse's last turn. He ran, he leapt, he flew, and landed—even further! As he stumbled to his feet, Luz reached him first.

'I knew you did it!' the German whispered. And as the officials measured the jump and confirmed an even newer world record, Luz took Jesse by the arm and led him towards the German crowd, lifting Jesse's arm in the air as a champion.

'Jesse Owens! Jesse Owens!' Luz shouted, as loudly as he could. Some of the crowd joined in. 'Jesse Owens! Jesse Owens!' Others took up the cry. Soon 100,000 Germans in Hitler's Olympic stadium were cheering the new champion. 'Jesse Owens! Jesse Owens! Jesse Owens! Jesse Owens!'

# Key points from the story

- In 1936, Hitler's Germany was a very difficult place to be if you weren't white. The Nazis believed that some ethnic and racial groups were superior to others, and that black people couldn't be as good as white people at anything. Hitler wanted these Games to prove it.
- Other Western countries were not free from prejudice, either. As Jesse Owens said afterwards, 'Although I wasn't invited to shake hands with Hitler, I wasn't invited to the White House to shake hands with the [American] President either.'
- Luz was taking a real risk when he chose to be Jesse's friend. Hitler had refused to meet Jesse, the winner of four Olympic gold medals.
- Luz later died serving his country as a soldier during World War II.

# Activities

## Religious Education: Key Stage 1

Can people who don't get on or don't like each other ever be friends? Is it possible to be kind to someone who isn't your friend to start with?

- Ask pupils to spread out around the room and individually mime a statue of how they would feel if people left them out or were unkind to them because of the way they looked or dressed or the colour of their skin. When they have posed in their statue, ask for one word that describes how they would feel.

    Repeat the activity, with pupils showing how their statue would look if people included them in a game or said kind words to them. What one word describes how they would feel?

- Luz was an unexpected friend. When Jesus was asked, 'Who is my neighbour?' he answered by telling the story of the good Samaritan, using a well-known 'enemy' to demonstrate what compassion was really all about. Read the original Bible story in Luke 10:30–37. Use puppets to retell the Bible story.

## Religious Education: Key Stage 2

- Find a photograph of US gold medallist Jesse Owens with German silver medallist Luz Long at the 1936 Olympic Games in Berlin, at **www.olympic.org**. (Search on the website for 'photo Jesse Luz'.) Jesse and Luz were 'enemies' who chose to be friends. In the Sermon on the Mount, Jesus said, 'Love your enemies and be good to them. Lend without expecting to be paid back. Then you will get a great reward, and you will be the true children of God in heaven' (Luke 6:35). What could this be saying about people who seem to be our enemies?

Create an illustrated poem or short story called 'The children of heaven' that explains your own thoughts and feelings about enemies and friends—and how people can change from one into the other.

- Luz was an unexpected friend. When Jesus was asked, 'Who is my neighbour?' he answered by telling the story of the good Samaritan, using a well-known 'enemy' to demonstrate what compassion was really all about. Read the original Bible story in Luke 10:30–37, then tell your own up-to-date version in a familiar setting, using characters we would now think of as being enemies of each other. If you want to be really clever, retell it in the form of a rap, manga strip-cartoon, puppet play, PowerPoint presentation with music and sound effects, or by using any other media.

## PSHE/Citizenship/Literacy

- 'It took a lot of courage for him to befriend me in front of Hitler… You can melt down all the medals and cups I have and they wouldn't be a plating on the 24-carat friendship that I felt for Luz Long at that moment.'

Jesse Owens said these words after being advised and congratulated by Luz Long at the 1936 Olympics.

What does 'friendship' mean? With a partner, produce the copy for a newspaper 'Wanted' advert for a good friend, exactly 20 words long, beginning like this: 'Wanted, a good friend—must be…'

- Jesse didn't have to trust Luz's advice in the qualifying round—but he did, and it was a good choice. However, not all 'friends' are good for us. On the internet there are social networking websites for 'friends' to share their news, likes, dislikes, and much more, but it is all done online. What do you think could be the dangers of 'making friends' like this? Research 'online safety' at **www.kidsmart.org.uk**, listing what you think are the best three pieces of advice offered—and why.

- Luz and Jesse kept in touch after the Berlin Olympics by writing letters. In his last letter, written as a soldier shortly before he died in battle, Luz asked Jesse to 'someday find my son… tell him about how things can be between men on this earth'. What do you think he meant? What had their friendship proved? Imagine that you are Jesse Owens, and many years later you discover the address of Luz's adult son, Karl. What would you want to tell him about the events of 1936? Write the letter.

# Haile Gebrselassie

*

# Haile Gebrselassie

*Long-distance runner, 10,000 metres*
*Competed in Atlanta, 1996; Sydney, 2000*

### Key themes

Discipline, Poverty, Prayer, Aspirations

### Key quote

*I'm not motivated by possessions or money.*
*I just love running. I do lots of things, but nothing*
*compares to running.*
HAILE GEBRSELASSIE

---

## Introduction

After checking for hazards on the floor, ask your pupils to remove their shoes (and socks? You decide...), walk around the room and then return to replace their footwear. Discuss in pairs what it felt like, and list the places where you might normally go barefoot.

Share some comments, pointing out that in some parts of the world it is normal for children their age to travel barefoot everywhere because shoes are too expensive.

To accompany the story below, if possible show some video footage of the 10,000 metre final at the Atlanta Olympics in 1996, which can be found in various places on the internet. The final section of Leslie Woodhead's 1999 film *Endurance* usefully replays elements of Haile's life story, intercut with race footage.

## Story retelling

The starting pistol was raised. Bang! The runners leapt forward, jockeying for position as they took the first curve, some thrusting forward, others holding back, calculating the energy needed to push ahead, hold a lead or keep it all in reserve for later. Quick decisions. Instant choices. Legs, muscles, lungs, bodies pounding around the track.

Haile held himself back. Ten thousand metres, 25 laps, was plenty of time for opponents to get tired, and he was used to running for miles at a time. So, as they settled into the first few laps, his mind wandered. 'I'm actually here in Atlanta at last,' he thought. 'Running in the Olympics for my country. My family.'

He remembered running barefoot on the way to school, ten miles daily, holding, cradling, his precious schoolbooks that offered so much hope for the poor farmer's son. Even now, he still bent his left arm like that when he ran.

Then there was that first school race, when he left everyone behind. The young boy entering the 1500 metres against lots of older boys—streaking ahead and beating them all with 100 metres to spare! The watching crowd had been ecstatic, rushing on to the track, carrying him on their shoulders, shouting, 'Haile! Haile!'

Running. He just loved it. The thrill of being alive, the mind and body and spirit working together at speed.

Round another curve. He saw a TV reporter talking to camera, and remembered listening on his father's radio to live reports of the 1980 Moscow Games, when another Ethiopian won the 10,000 metres. 'And now it's my turn to try,' he thought. 'My turn to show the world what we can do.'

His father had wanted him to stay at home and help with the farm. He remembered the arguments. 'What can running get you? I need you here!' But the old man had finally agreed to it, bless him. 'He'll be watching me now on the village's only television,' Haile thought, 'as I run for Ethiopia.'

A few more laps. Haile slowly worked his way forward through the pack of other runners. He could remember moving to Addis, the nation's capital, running along the tracks and foothills that sur-rounded the city, and being spotted by a running coach. 'You need a team,' said the coach. 'Do you really want to run? Join our training programme.'

All those exercise routines. All that discipline. All those hours spent on the move, improving his endurance—the will to win that lasts for miles and miles.

More laps. Half-way. He'd been selected for international competitions. Antwerp. Stuttgart. Budapest. Gothenburg. Victories—was that what it was all about? Getting medals? He also remembered walking into church, kneeling, and offering his running skills to God. 'If I win in Atlanta,' he'd thought, 'I'll bring back my medal and leave it here in the church, as a sign.' Not as a bargain. Not to buy God's approval. He'd worked hard, but without God all his efforts would be useless.

Not long now to the finish. Haile was second in the pack. He'd passed the others, but there was still the Kenyan runner out in front. A bell rang somewhere, signalling one final lap to go. Now it was time! Haile powered forward, overtaking the Kenyan, pushing ahead. But could he keep the pace?

He was in front, but for how long? Haile glanced back. No. Keep looking ahead. Nearly there! Keep going! The finishing line's ahead! Crowds are cheering. I'm nearly there, don't slow down.

Over the line at last. 'I've finally done it,' he thought. 'For my family, for my people, for my God. I've won.'

He bent over to catch his breath, felt people patting him on the back, shaking his hand. Someone gave him a flag to hold, the flag of Ethiopia, his homeland. Haile jogged to the grass verge, took off his running shoes and did one more circuit of the stadium, waving to the crowd, proudly carrying his nation's flag and wearing a wide smile.

And at the medal award ceremony, when they played the Ethiopian national anthem to celebrate Haile's win, he was weeping—with joy.

## Key points from the story

- Haile was born and raised in a single-roomed hut on a farm in a very poor part of the world. As he grew up, Ethiopia experienced drought, famine and civil war.
- This background, and the high altitude, helped to make Haile tough. He was used to making long journeys on foot to fetch water or get to school.
- Running is now a high-profile popular sport in Ethiopia and carries a lot of national pride—especially when Ethiopians race Kenyans!
- Haile's successes in running won him a lot of prize money, which he used to build up several successful businesses, employ hundreds of local people, and fund the building of schools and hospitals.

## Activities

### Religious Education: Key Stage 1

Haile was a man who believed in God, and he believed it was important to pray.

- Together, write a prayer that Haile may have prayed before or after his race.
- The Ethiopian cross is an important symbol in the Orthodox Church and is highly symmetrical in design. Print off a copy of this cross for each pupil from the internet. Pupils can decorate the cross using patterns that are the same on both sides.

## Religious Education: Key Stage 2

As an Orthodox Christian, Haile had strong positive beliefs that affected his sporting performance. He said:

*I have to work hard, but without God, all my efforts are useless.*

*When you believe in something, you believe in yourself as well. I believe in God.*

*I go to a church and pray, not just to pray to God, but at the same time to pray for myself. Your body is always ready to do what you ask it. That's why believing is very important. I am a religious person. My family taught me how to pray.*

To reproduce these quotes, download the pdf file at www. barnabasinschools.org.uk/9781841017426/

- Write a prayer that you think Haile might have prayed in church before going to compete in the Atlanta Games. Then write the prayer you think he might have said when he returned, carrying his gold medal. Illustrate this with a picture of an Ethiopian cross (examples of which can be found via an internet image search).

- The Ethiopian cross is an important symbol in the Orthodox Church and is highly symmetrical in design. You can make the basic shape by folding a square piece of paper in four and then cutting it similarly to the way in which we make 'snowflake' designs. It can be decorated with silver paper and other materials to achieve a 'jewelled' effect.

For more background and lesson material relating to this and other world cross motifs, see Martyn Payne and Betty Pedley's book *A-cross the World*, published by Barnabas in Schools and available from your bookshop or from www. barnabasinschools.org.uk/

## PSHE/Citizenship/Literacy

- Find a picture of the Ethiopian flag. Why do you think Haile was waving it and carrying it so proudly after his race? Draw and label the flag (or make it out of coloured sticky paper) and add thought bubbles around its edge, to show what you think Haile's thoughts would have been, both at that moment after the race and during the medal ceremony.

- Ethiopia is known as a 'developing nation', with most people there having a lower standard of living than people in the West. But Haile gets cross at the way some people judge his country unfairly.

  'The thing that really offends me,' he says, 'is that the most important value in the 21st century is how much money you have. They say the most important thing in the world is to be rich. But money is not everything!'

Read Haile's story again, listing under your Ethiopian flag what he might think the most important things really are. Tick the ones you especially agree with.

• Some Ethiopians would like Haile to go into politics when he stops running. He says, 'If I were prime minister, I would send everyone to school. Education is all. That is what I would love to do for this country: educate it.'

Send My Friend To School is a charity, supported by many schools in the UK, that campaigns to allow more children around the world to have an education. Visit **www.sendmyfriend.org** to find out more, then design a bookmark or lapel badge with words and symbols that sum up the charity's key message. Consider planning a charity event to raise money for this cause.

Haile's advice to anyone thinking of getting into sport is:

*You need three things to win: discipline, hard work and, before everything maybe, commitment. No one will make it without those three. Sport teaches you that.*

*It is not enough just to win the race, it is how you handle the lessons, how you improve. Some athletes, after they have won something, because they are not disciplined, they don't make the most of it.*

*I am not hungry for success, I am hungry for running. I am disciplined. Sometimes when I meet people and they say, 'What do I have to do to be like you?' I say, 'Look, sport has to come from inside.' You can't look at someone and say, 'I want to be like you.' The desire has to be yours.*

To reproduce these quotes, download the pdf file at www.barnabasinschools.org.uk/9781841017426/

- Where do you think Haile learned these beliefs? Try to sum up his key ideas in as few words as possible. What pictures or symbols would convey these thoughts? Use them to create a T-shirt design that includes at least one positive image connected to Ethiopia.

# Eric Liddell

1924

Eric Liddell

# Eric Liddell

*Runner, 200 metres and 400 metres*
*Competed in Paris, 1924*

## Key themes

Discipline, Principles, Inspiration, Adaptability

## Key quote

*I just don't like to be beaten.*
ERIC LIDDELL

---

## Introduction

Are there some things that are so special to you, so precious, that you will hold to them no matter what? Explain that many people have a personal core belief that gives them a strength and sense of direction for their life. But what happens if that core belief comes up against something that refuses to recognise it? What do you sacrifice? Many people have had to give up all sorts of good things to follow their beliefs.

To accompany the story below, you might wish to show a clip from the Oscar-winning 1981 film *Chariots of Fire*, such as the footage of the 400m race.

## Story retelling

The British team were baffled when they heard about it. What was wrong? Why couldn't their best sprinter run his race? 'It's for the Olympics!' they said. 'You're one of the fastest men in the world!'

Eric Liddell wouldn't have it. 'Because that race is on the Lord's Day. It's the sabbath. I'm not running on a Sunday.'

The Paris Olympics were a few months away, and the race details had just been released. Eric's best event was the 100 metre sprint, but the qualifying finals for the 100 metres, the 4 x 100 metre relay and the 4 x 400 metre relay would all take place on a Sunday—the Christian sabbath.

Eric never ran on the sabbath, even though 100 metres was his best distance by far.

'So what are you going to do?' asked his team mates.

'Train for the 400 metres—I've done well in it before.'

'But it's not your best event.'

Eric wouldn't be moved. By the time of the Paris Olympics, he was as ready as he'd ever be. But would his beliefs cost him the gold medal? Many saw him as the sprinter who had given up his chance to win the 100 metres for his country. Had he done the right thing? Yes—but some newspapers had even called him a traitor, and that hurt.

It was Friday morning, the day of the 400 metre final. He'd trained hard for it and qualified well, but already the summer weather was stifling. Some were calling this stadium 'the furnace' because of the baking heat. The runners lined up, each of them crouching down with a trowel to shape their own particular starting line, digging out a small pit for each foot to give maximum thrust when they heard the starting pistol.

Eric was thinking hard. He wanted to win, but he'd sacrificed the 100 metres. Was it possible to do it in a different event? The speed was different, the timing was different. All that training, all that sacrifice.

At the stadium, he'd opened a note given him at his hotel—and read these words: 'In the old book it says, "He that honours me, I will honour." Wishing you the best of success always.' An encouragement from the British team physio.

Eric smiled at the memory, then turned back to his preparations. From somewhere in the stadium, he could hear bagpipes, the sound of Scotland, his home. Now he was ready. The trowels were collected and he followed his normal custom of walking along the starting line, shaking hands with his opponents, then returned to his lane and crouched down, staring ahead. There were just two straights and a curve on this track. He was on the outside lane, and would have to get to the curve first.

The starter gave his final instructions. 'Get set.' The runners silently tensed up, straining to hear the sound. Crack! went the pistol. Up, out, running as fast as possible, pushing forward. Eric was streaking ahead, like a sprinter. It was the only thing he knew. Striding out, knees pumping. Pushing, pushing along the straight towards the first curve, leaving the others behind. He was round the curve, but would he run out of steam? You can't sprint 400 metres. No one can.

But he kept running. The others were catching up, gaining on him, getting closer. It was the final straight.

'Those who honour me, I will honour.' Eric put everything into the last 100 metres; the power was coming from somewhere. Head back, chin forward, mouth open, knees jumping, arms waving in the air.

Pushing forward again... pushing... and over the line. Finished.

First. He'd won. 400 metres. 47.6 seconds. A new Olympic record. Unbelievable!

Eric collected his gold medal, but didn't stay in the stadium for long. He went back to his hotel to clean up. That Sunday, he was going to be preaching in a Paris church, and he needed time to prepare his words and think. The newspapers that had said so many horrible things about him were now calling him a marvel, but what they said didn't matter. He had other things to do that were much more important.

Eric Liddell

# Key points from the story

- As a Christian, Eric had refused to compete in his best events (100 metre sprint and relay) because it would mean running the qualifying heats on a Sunday, something that went against his core beliefs.
- Instead, he trained for the 200 metres and 400 metres, which needed a different training and strategy (although he still ran them like a 100 metre sprint).
- He won a bronze medal for the 200 metres and gold for his famous 400 metre run.
- Eric was born in China to Scottish parents who were Christian missionaries, and after the Olympics he was soon training to be a missionary himself. He spent most of his adult life in China, looking after people and teaching them about Jesus, and died there.

# Activities

## Religious Education: Key Stage 1

In the Bible (Matthew 4:1–11), we read about Jesus facing temptations.

*The Holy Spirit led Jesus into the desert, so that the devil could test him. After Jesus had gone without eating for forty days and nights, he was very hungry. Then the devil came to him and said, 'If you are God's Son, tell these stones to turn into bread.'*

*Jesus answered, 'The Scriptures say: "No one can live only on food. People need every word that God has spoken."'*

*Next, the devil took Jesus to the holy city and made him stand on the highest part of the temple. The devil said, 'If you are God's Son, jump off. The Scriptures say: "God will give his angels orders about you. They will catch you in their arms, and you won't hurt your feet on the stones."'*

*Jesus answered, 'The Scriptures also say, "Don't try to test the Lord your God!"'*

*Finally, the devil took Jesus up on a very high mountain and showed him all the kingdoms on earth and their power. The devil said to him, 'I will give all this to you, if you will bow down and worship me.'*

*Jesus answered, 'Go away Satan! The Scriptures say: "Worship the Lord your God and serve only him."'*

*Then the devil left Jesus, and angels came to help him.*

Jesus was tempted to use miracles for his own benefit—for example, turning stones into bread when he hadn't eaten and was hungry—but he resisted. Eric Liddell was put under a lot of pressure to run on a Sunday and was even called a 'traitor' when he refused. He must have been tempted to go against what he believed to please everyone else and compete for his medal. We all have times when other people try to persuade us or tempt us to do things that we know are not right.

• Think of times when we are tempted to make a wrong choice or not do the right thing. Talk with the children about why we should or shouldn't do these things.

Write some of the ideas on a piece of paper and ask the children to draw happy or sad faces, depending on whether they think they are right or wrong (or straight faces if they are not sure).

# Religious Education: Key Stage 2

- Sometimes our personal beliefs can clash with the beliefs of others. Muslim athletes from many nations may find it difficult competing in international sporting events during Ramadan because, during that time, a devout Muslim doesn't take in food or water during daylight hours. This causes problems for athletes competing, especially in summer when the daylight hours are long. Eric faced a similar problem about running on the Christian sabbath. What feelings experienced by Eric in 1924 would be similar to those of modern Muslim athletes?

  Draw two faces on a page, labelled 'Eric Liddell 1924' and 'Muslim athlete today'. Write some thought bubbles for both of them in the run-up to the Games, with sentences inside beginning, 'I wish…', 'I believe…' and 'I hope…' Would any of their thoughts be similar? Why?

- In 1991, a memorial headstone was unveiled at the former prison camp in China where Eric died. Apart from his personal details, it includes these words from the Bible: 'They shall mount up with wings as eagles; they shall run and not be weary' (Isaiah 40:31). What do you think these words are saying about the life of Eric

Liddell as a runner and as a Christian? Looking ahead, what words would you choose to have inscribed on your own headstone to sum up the way you would like your life to be remembered?

Design what you think Eric's memorial would look like. Then, if you have time, design your own.

- Eric didn't want to run on the Christian sabbath (Sunday) because he firmly believed it to be a special day dedicated to God. Nowadays, Sunday in this country is treated by many as just another day for work, shopping or leisure. What do you think about that? Should there be a special day that's different from the others?

  Keep Sunday Special is a campaign group who argue that Sundays need to be much less busy. With a partner, research their reasons at **www.keepsundayspecial.org. uk/Web** and sum up their main arguments in 50 words or less.

  What would Keep Sunday Special's opponents say against their arguments? Use these thoughts to create a summary of the debate, and in conclusion give your own opinion about how Sundays should be used.

- Many years later, in China, Eric was looking after some teenagers in a prison camp, and spent a lot of time giving them positive things to do in a very difficult place. He was still passionate about not playing games on a Sunday. Some of the teenagers wanted to have a hockey match on a Sunday, boys against girls, and organised it themselves—but it turned into a fight because there was no referee. On the following Sunday, Eric came out to referee for them. Remember that he had refused to run on a Sunday for an Olympic gold medal. What does this later story tell you about him? Why do you think he broke the rule he had kept for years?

Two of his favourite Bible passages were 1 Corinthians 13:1–13 and Matthew 5:3–12.

*What if I could speak all languages of humans and of angels? If I did not love others, I would be nothing more than a noisy gong or a clanging cymbal. What if I could prophesy and understand all secrets and all knowledge? And what if I had faith that moved mountains? I would be nothing, unless I loved others. What if I gave away all that I owned and let myself be burned alive? I would gain nothing, unless I loved others.*

*Love is kind and patient, never jealous, boastful, proud, or rude. Love isn't selfish or quick tempered. It doesn't keep a record of wrongs that others do. Love rejoices in the truth, but not in evil. Love is always supportive, loyal, hopeful, and trusting. Love never fails!*

*Everyone who prophesies will stop, and unknown languages will no longer be spoken. All that we know will be forgotten. We don't know everything, and our prophecies are not complete. But what is perfect will some day appear, and what isn't perfect will then disappear.*

*When we were children, we thought and reasoned as children do. But when we grew up, we stopped our childish ways. Now all we can see of God is like a cloudy picture in a mirror. Later we will see him face to face. We don't*

*know everything, but then we will, just as God completely
understands us. For now there are faith, hope, and love. But of
these three, the greatest is love.*
1 CORINTHIANS 13:1–13

*God blesses those people who depend only on him. They
belong to the kingdom of heaven!*

*God blesses those people who grieve. They will find
comfort!*

*God blesses those people who are humble. The earth will
belong to them!*

*God blesses those people who want to obey him more than
to eat or drink. They will be given what they want!*

*God blesses those people who are merciful. They will be
treated with mercy!*

*God blesses those people whose hearts are pure. They will
see him!*

*God blesses those people who make peace. They will be
called his children!*

*God blesses those people who are treated badly for doing
right. They belong to the kingdom of heaven.*

*God will bless you when people insult you, ill-treat you,
and tell all kinds of evil lies about you because of me. Be
happy and excited! You will have a great reward in heaven.
People did these same things to the prophets who lived long
ago.*
MATTHEW 5:3–12

To reproduce these quotes, download the pdf file at www.
barnabasinschools.org.uk/9781841017426/

- Choose one of these passages, draw a hockey stick, and copy out any verses that you think would have spoken to Eric as he was wondering what to do about the teenagers.

# PSHE/Citizenship/Literacy

- Ask the class to think of things or people that are important or special to them. Would they be willing to give up other things for those important things or people? Eric Liddell was willing to do that.

  Provide a selection of word cards with pictures of objects such as a TV, Bike, DS, Wii and any other material items. As a class, sort the items into those that are considered to be important or special and those that are not.

  Repeat the activity using word cards showing non-material items such as Family, Friends, Love, Care, Pets, Sharing, School. Discuss what makes something important or special.

- Play a 'choices' mime game. Ask pupils to spread out around the room and mime the following scenario. They have been out playing and come in feeling really hungry. They see some freshly baked cakes on the table. They know the cakes are for tea, but they look really nice and the children are hungry. Should they take a cake? Freeze the mime as they reach out a hand towards the cakes.

Ask pupils to give one reason why they should take a cake and one reason why they shouldn't. Now ask them to make a decision: are they going to take one or not? Discuss what it means to be disciplined enough to do what is right, even when it isn't easy.

• Before... and after. Imagine you are a very patriotic sportswriter reporting for one of the major newspapers in 1924. You know that Great Britain's best hope for a gold medal has refused to run in the 100 metres, for religious reasons. Instead, he is running in the 400 metres, which is not his best event. What would you think and say about Eric? Write two 'opinion pieces' for the newspaper for the day before the 400 metre race (Thursday 10 July) and the evening after the race (Friday 11 July). Your second piece might be rather different from your first!

Eric's place in the 100 metre race was taken by Harold Abrahams, who ran it on 7 July, winning a gold medal. This was a few days before Eric's 400 metre race. How might that change the way you write both reports? Would a reporter be more or less pleased about Eric's decision?

# Lilo Ljubisic

1988–2000

Lilo Ljubisic

\*

# Lilo Ljubisic

*Discus and shot put*
*Competed in Seoul, 1988; Barcelona, 1992;*
*Atlanta, 1996; Sydney, 2000*

## Key themes

Determination, Dedication, Disability, Equality,
Inequality

## Key quote

*There are many things in your life that will catch*
*your eye, but only a few will catch your heart.*
*Pursue those.*
LILO LJUBISIC

---

## Introduction

Ask pupils to discuss in pairs what choices they had to make
before arriving at school this morning. Then ask them to
imagine how those choices might be affected if they were
disabled in some way—such as being partially sighted,
hearing impaired or having to use a wheelchair.

## Story retelling

Lilo couldn't believe what Mrs Henderson had just said.

'Volleyball?' asked Lilo. 'You actually want me to play volleyball? But I can hardly see to hit the ball!'

'Don't rule yourself out because of that,' the PE teacher replied. 'I think you could be a great server. You've got the height for it, and I see you estimating distances all the time as you move around school. I think you could have the muscle and skill to be rather good at volleyball if you practise.'

It seemed a crazy idea. Lilo had suffered from poor eyesight for years, ever since a doctor had given her the wrong treatment for a common childhood illness. Now, normal light hurt her eyes. She had to walk under a big black umbrella on bright days, wearing a baseball cap with a wide brim, with large sunglasses to block out the glare. When reading at school, she had to hold the books so close to her face that her nose was often smudged from the ink. As for PE lessons, she normally sat out, preferring study in the library to sitting on the sidelines, watching other kids participate in activities she could only dream of playing.

But volleyball? Mrs Henderson was insistent. So, after being given a crash course in serving, and after Mrs Henderson had worked out a way to help her estimate the heights and distances of a volleyball court, Lilo continued practising against the gym wall and in the backyard of her home until she got the serve just right. She would cradle the ball in her left hand, drawing back the right at waist height, punching the ball up and over to land just inside the opponent's side of the net. Practice makes perfect, even if you're visually impaired.

Two weeks later, Mrs Henderson organised a volleyball game for the PE class, saying that this time Lilo would be playing too, but only as a server for her team. (Usually, volleyball players switch positions throughout the game.) The two captains picked teams and Lilo was, naturally, picked last. But then it was her team's turn to begin. Lilo took her place as server on the court and was handed the ball. Ready? She held the ball, swung… and served. Thud! The sound of a ball hitting the ground.

'What happened? Where did it go?' asked Lilo.

Someone shouted, 'One nothing. An ace!' Lilo had gained a point! The ball had sailed over the net and hit the opponents' side of the court so fast that no one could touch it. Lilo served again, scoring another point. And another point. And another. Lilo sent 15 straight serves sailing over the net to win the game for her team with hardly anybody else touching the ball—except to fetch it and bring it back to her.

So a new life began for the teenager. Lilo's mother had always told her that God had a special plan for her life, and sport began opening doors. At university, Lilo took up goalball, a team sport designed for the blind, and was soon playing in competitions. By the age of 23, she was playing goalball for the Canadian Paralympic team.

After that came an interest in field athletics. She decided to specialise in the throwing events, concentrating on shot put and discus. It was hard work, but she was determined that her disability wouldn't get in the way of doing her best. A team coach provided guidance, training and fitness routines. Lilo rediscovered the Christian faith that she'd had in her early years and was baptised. She also married. More doors were opening.

Over the next few years, Lilo won gold, silver and bronze medals at the Paralympics in Seoul, Barcelona, Atlanta and Sydney, and set new world records for throwing the shot put and discus. It wasn't easy, and there were lots of difficulties to face and more choices to make, but sport had shown her how to face challenges and overcome them, too. It was all about having a belief in your own value and your ability to choose. And so much of it had started all those years ago, with someone who had first chosen to believe in her.

# Key points from the story

- Lilo was born sighted, but a childhood illness and poor medical treatment led to many years of increasing blindness and pain.
- At school in both Yugoslavia and Canada, Lilo experienced a lot of teasing and bullying because her disability made her look different from other children.

- As a young adult, Lilo discovered the power of choice. She didn't have to accept the limits that others placed on her because she was blind.
- Sport opened up a whole new set of possibilities for Lilo. She is now retired from athletics but still campaigns for the rights of children facing difficulties like hers, and uses her story to encourage young people to make the most of the choices before them.

# Activities

## Religious Education: Key Stage 1

Psalm 23 is one of the best-known psalms in the Bible. It talks about having a shepherd (God) who will guide people even in the most difficult and frightening times.

*Even if I go through the deepest darkness, I will not be afraid, Lord, for you are with me. Your shepherd's rod and staff protect me.*
PSALM 23:4 (GNB)

The sheep wouldn't be able to go along some of those paths without the shepherd guiding them, because it would be too dangerous, but they trust their shepherd to lead them safely along. Lilo had many hard times in her life, and her faith in God helped her through.

- Draw a picture of a sheep walking along a very dangerous path. Then think of a difficult time you have been through. Write it under your picture and then write who helped you through that time. If you have a friend going through a difficult time, how might you be able to help them?

# Religious Education: Key Stage 2

Here is some advice from Lilo for young people.

*First, challenge yourself to do the best you can with the talents with which you are blessed. It is very important to set goals and dream big. Being able to visualise your dream brings you closer to your achievement—especially in my case, since I'm blind. Second, grasp the power and strength in teamwork. No one stands alone. Find people who will support your dream and help you to make it a reality. Third, focus on what you can do, and not on what you can't.*

*Faith is the basis of my life, the sustaining power to overcome adversity. In the shadowy, cold valleys, we realise we aren't self-sustaining—and need to lean on God's love and mercy.*

*You can do it. With courage, commitment, and hard work, you can achieve your goals. You have the choice.*

To reproduce these quotes, download the pdf file at www.barnabasinschools.org.uk/9781841017426/

- In the Bible, someone wrote, 'Faith means being sure of the things we hope for and knowing that something

is real even if we do not see it' (Hebrews 11:1, NCV).
Copy out this verse and draw Lilo's sunglasses. Lilo's
Christian faith helps her to believe in herself and her
abilities. It gives her an inner strength. Now draw
yourself on a page. Around the picture, draw or list the
things that make you strong. Think especially about
the things that help you to believe in yourself and your
ability to handle challenges. Who do you trust to help
you? If you wish, copy out a suitable quote from Lilo
that you agree with, or a good piece of advice from
somebody that gave you inner strength.

# PSHE/Citizenship/Literacy

- Lilo says, 'We are the only beings on this planet that
  have the power of choice.' List 20 choices you will have
  to make today that an animal (such as a dog or cat)
  can't make. Look at your list again. Put a star next to the
  ones that might be important in a week's time. Circle
  the ones that could be important for you in a year's
  time. Underline the ones that might be important in
  five years' time. Discuss your list with a partner. Over
  the next year, what are the most important choices you
  might have to make, and why? Write about them.

- Lilo says, 'Years ago, I would show up at local all-
  comers tournaments. The event organisers would tell
  me I wasn't welcome. That kind of rejection marked me;
  it served as the impetus for me to make change. I have
  bruises all over my body from hitting barriers. But once

I broke through those, I could look back and see there
was a hole. Now, 20 years later, there's no trace there
was ever a wall there.'

Draw a figure of Lilo standing next to a high wall
made up of large bricks. On the bricks, write some of
the excuses people might have made when telling Lilo
that she couldn't compete in an athletics competition
for shot put or discus. Nearby, draw a bulldozer. By the
bulldozer, write some of the answers that Lilo might
have given.

- Lilo was born in Yugoslavia, where, at that time, there
was no special provision for partially sighted children,
apart from a special school 100 miles away from her
family home. Her parents campaigned to get her instead
into a local school that would accept a child with special
needs. In the end, the family emigrated to Canada
to find a school that would give Lilo the support she
needed. Using a map of your own school, think about
how your school is designed, built and run. How has
it been adapted to help people with special needs and
disabilities? Start by thinking about wheelchair access
for entrances, exits and doors, including ramps. Are
there other things too? Could you spot something
else that needs doing, and suggest (or even design) a
solution for it? For example, think of the entrance hall
and the playground.

- Disabled sports (also known as Para sports or Adaptive
sports) and competitions are on offer in many places

these days. Research some of them, choose one that appeals to you and create a poster explaining what it's about and celebrating its achievements.

# Assemblies and Collective Worship

*

# Collective Worship: Preparing to do our best

## Aim

To think about the things we need to do, to prepare to do our best in sport and in living the way God wants us to live.

## Props

- A pre-arranged volunteer dressed in PE kit if possible.
- Dressing-up props that are inappropriate for racing—for example, large wellies, raincoat and umbrella; or flip flops, sun hat and sunglasses; or flippers, swimming hat and goggles.

## Bible passage

So we must get rid of everything that slows us down, especially the sin that just won't let go. And we must be determined to run the race that is ahead of us. We must keep our eyes on Jesus, who leads us and makes our faith complete.

HEBREWS 12:1B–2A

# How can we prepare to do our best?

*Talk about the things you need to do to be prepared for a race, asking the children for suggestions (for example, training, practising, warming up, knowing about your opponents, eating healthily, drinking water, buying the right gear, wearing the right clothes).*

There is a boy/girl in school who has been preparing for a big race, and today's the day! He/she will be racing against lots of other children and has been doing many of the things you've just suggested, to prepare.

*Bring out your volunteer and ask them to demonstrate some of their warm-up exercises: stretching, running on the spot, and so on. Ask the other children:*

How do you think they're going to do? Do you think they'll win? Do they look as though they've prepared well?

Now, I think [name] is looking great and is going to do really well, so I thought I'd give them a bit of a helping hand. *(Turning to volunteer)* I have some things here to help you. Would you like them?

*Pick up a bag with one of the inappropriate sets of clothing and hand it to them.*

I've been thinking it may rain/it may be very hot/ you may need to run through a river... so I've got you some extra clothes in case that happens. Here you are; put them on.

*Encourage your volunteer to put them on.*

These will really help you out. You're bound to win the race now. [Name] will win now, won't he/she?

*The other children are bound to point out that they will not and that the things you've given them will slow them down. Enter into a short dialogue about this.*

Oh yes, I suppose you're right. These things will slow them down, and they won't win the race if they're slowed down by them, will they?

*Ask your volunteer to take off the extra clothes and sit down.*

## Application

There's a verse in the Bible that says, 'So we must get rid of everything that slows us down, especially the sin that just won't let go. And we must be determined to run the race that is ahead of us.' Christians believe that this is talking about how we run God's race, which means living the way God wants us to live, showing love and respect to other people and spending our time on good and positive things. There are many things that may stop us living the way he wants us to and may spoil our lives but, as [name] got rid of the things that would slow him/her down, so we should get rid of the things that might spoil the way we run God's race. Jesus has already run the race and finished it well, so he can help us to do the same.

# Reflection

Think about the things that can slow you down and stop you from doing the right things in your life. *(If there is time, ask for examples of things that may slow us down and stop us doing the right things, or ask the teachers to use circle time to share some of the right choices that children have made.)*

Let's think about how you can get rid of those things and run the race of life in the right way. Maybe you might want to ask God to help you.

I am going to say a prayer, and, if you agree with what I am saying, you might want to say 'Amen' at the end, which means 'I agree'.

**PRAYER**

*Lord God, thank you that you have run the race of life ahead of us and that you know it's hard to do the right thing sometimes. Thank you that you want to help us to make the right choices and live in a way that makes you happy. We pray that you will. Amen*

*

# Interactive story: David and Goliath

You can perform this story in various ways, depending on what works best for you and your school. One way (as shown in the following story script) is to choose several children to play the different characters, either reading the lines or miming the story as you read. Split the rest of the children into two halves down the middle of the room. One side will play the Israelites, while the other side play the Philistines. At certain points, they will taunt each other with the following words:

**Philistines:** *(as if chanting 'Na-na-na, na-na!' and pointing with raised arms)* We're going to beat you!
**Israelites:** *(looking worried, pretending to bite fingernails, using the same chant)* Oh no, you're no-ot!

David was an ordinary shepherd-boy from an ordinary family (although the family was quite large: he had seven older brothers). While he was looking after his dad's sheep, I think David probably used to get quite bored. Sometimes he wrote songs and played them on his harp. Sometimes he practised with his slingshot. He would put a stone in the centre of a small strip of leather, spin it round and round, gaining speed, and then let go of one end. The stone would fly through the air so fast that you couldn't see it go. David, like many other shepherd-boys, became a really good shot, and sometimes he had to use his sling to scare away bears, wolves or even lions.

When our story starts, some of David's brothers were away fighting in King Saul's army: they were the Israelites. The battle was against their enemy, the Philistines. The Philistines were camped on one side of the valley and the Israelites on the opposite side.

Now, the Philistines had a secret weapon in their army: it was a man! This man was so big and so tall that everyone called him 'The Giant'. (He wasn't a fairytale giant, of course, just a really, really big man.) His name was Goliath, and Goliath would come out of the Philistine camp and yell across the valley to the Israelites in his fiercest roar of a voice:

**Goliath:** Come on, you Israelites, send down your champion! You're not scared, are you? You must have someone who will take me on!

The Philistines loved this, and would stand behind Goliath and taunt the Israelites:

**Philistines: We're going to beat you!**

None of the Israelites wanted to take on this big man. They were all terrified, but tried to respond bravely:

**Israelites: Oh no, you're no-ot!**

Secretly, though, they thought the Philistines *would* win!

**Philistines: We're going to beat you!**
**Israelites: Oh no, you're no-ot!**

David was at home on the hillside, looking after the sheep as usual, and he didn't know any of this was going on, but how he wished that he was old enough to be fighting with his brothers in the battle. One day, David's dad, Jesse, called him.

**Jesse:** David, I want you to do a job for me.
**David:** OK, Dad.
**Jesse:** I want you to go and visit your brothers in the army.
**David:** Yes! *(Punches the air)*
**Jesse:** See how they're getting on, and take them some food in case they're getting hungry.
**David:** OK, Dad.

*Jesse gives various items to David, who soon gets overloaded.*

**Jesse:** Take them some sandwiches, and bread and cheese, and cake. There's some fruit and veg, and here's some fresh water. Oh… and a pasty and some pickle. Now hurry along, off you go!

David set off, carrying all the goodies for his brothers. He arrived at the Israelite camp just in time to see

Goliath come out across the valley with his usual taunt.

**Goliath:** Come on, you Israelites, send down your champion! You're not scared, are you? You must have someone who will take me on!

**Philistines: We're going to beat you!**
**Israelites: Oh no, you're no-ot!**

David met his brothers, carrying all the goodies, and, like most little brothers, came out with loads of questions.

**David:** What's going on? Who's that big man? Why is there so much shouting? Who's going to take him on, then? Why hasn't anyone sorted him out yet? Where's the toilet? Oh, and Dad's sent these.

One of his brothers replied as many older brothers reply to younger brothers.

**Brother:** What are you doing here, and why are you asking silly questions? Go back home to Dad and practise playing 'Baa, baa, black sheep' on your recorder or something useful!

But David wasn't put off.

**David:** No! Who's going to take him on? You shouldn't be scared of him. He may be big but we've got God on our side and he will protect us. Oh... *I'll* go and sort him out, then!

Even though his brothers were trying to send him back home, David headed off to see the king. He arrived at the palace and was taken to see King Saul.

**David:** Whoa! I like your crown!

(Well, he probably didn't say that, but you never know!)

**David:** King Saul, I have come to talk to you about the big man they call 'The Giant'. No one seems to want to take him on, but, Your Majesty, I will take him on.

King Saul looked him up and down and chuckled.

**Saul:** Well, young man, it's a very noble offer, but you can't take him on. He's so huge and you're so small.

**David:** That doesn't matter. I'll take him on—I'm not afraid of him. I've got God on my side and I'll go in the power of the Lord.

David went on to tell the king how he'd seen off wolves and even killed lions and bears. Despite Saul's reluctance to let him do it, there was no one else. Saul couldn't persuade anyone else to go, so eventually he agreed to let David try.

**Saul:** OK, you can go.

But then King Saul made a mistake that many adults would be tempted to make: he tried to give David things that he didn't need.

**Saul:** But if you're going, I insist that you take this. Here's my armour.

David tried to put it on, but he nearly fell over because it was so heavy.

**Saul:** And my sword and shield.

David couldn't lift them!

**Saul:** And my helmet.

David tried to put it on, but his head nearly fell off!

**David:** These things are no good for me *(handing them back)*. You're nearly twice my size and they're way too big. They'll just slow me down and get in the way. Thanks, but I don't need your weapons or your armour. God will give me all I need—I'm going in the power of the Lord.

As David headed out, King Saul looked defeated. David arrived in the valley just as Goliath came out with his usual taunt.

**Goliath:** Come on, you Israelites, send down your champion! You're not scared, are you? You must have someone who will take me on!

**Philistines: We're going to beat you!**
**Israelites: Oh no, you're no-ot!**

(Most of the Israelites still thought he would.) David spoke up.

**David:** I will take you on!

Goliath peered across the valley and laughed. The Philistines laughed. The Israelites trembled.

**Goliath:** You can't take me on. You're so small, I can hardly see you! Is this a joke?

**David:** I'm no joke, and I'm going to fight you. I'm not afraid of you! I've got God on my side and I'm coming in the power of the Lord.

David quietly bent down and picked up five stones. He put four in his pocket and one in his sling. He began to spin the sling around, gaining speed. At just the right moment, he let go of one end of the sling, and the stone flew through the air so fast, like a bullet from a gun, that no one saw it coming. It hit Goliath right in the middle of his forehead and Goliath fell down to the ground with a thud. He was dead!

Just so that everyone knew Goliath was dead, David ran over to him, picked up his sword and, with one huge swing, cut off his head—YUK! The Israelites cheered.

**Israelites: We have beaten you!**
**Philistines: Aaaaaaargh!**

David had won. The Philistines were defeated! And it was all because he put his trust in God. He could have put his trust in King Saul's armour and weapons, but he knew those would be no good and would slow him down. He relied on God instead.

To reproduce this script, download the pdf file at:
www.barnabasinschools.org.uk/9781841017426/

# Reflection

Think about the things that can slow you down and stop you from doing the right things in your life. (*If there is time, ask for examples of things that may slow us down and stop us doing the right things, or ask the teachers to use circle time to share some of the right choices that children have made.*)

Let's think about how you can get rid of those things and run the race of life in the right way. Maybe you want to ask God to help you.

I am going to say a prayer, and, if you agree with what I am saying, you might want to say 'Amen' at the end, which means 'I agree'.

## PRAYER

*Lord God, thank you that you have run the race of life ahead of us and that you know it's hard to do the right thing sometimes. Thank you that you want to help us to make the right choices and live in a way that makes you happy. We pray that you will. Amen*

*

# Reflective story:
# The race that lasts a
# lifetime

## You will need:

- Three boxes of different heights (ultimately to form a podium). For good storage effect they could fit into one another, as supplied by Hobbycraft and others
- Sweat bands and a cross
- Baton and group picture/model of church building
- Whistle and Bible
- Piece of green felt to build on

## Thoughts and questions

We are going to think about what it takes for sportspeople to prepare to participate in their chosen sport—how they have to train to do their best—and we will consider that Christians are in training themselves to follow their faith.

I wonder what is the biggest sporting event you have been to. It might have been the Olympics or a football match, or something in your local park. And what is the biggest sporting event you have taken part in? It might be a football tournament, or a tennis match or a school sports day.

*As you speak, roll out the green felt, imagining a sports field.*

Being a Christian is like being in a race. Paul writes about it in the Bible. It's a race that lasts a lifetime!

*Bring out the first, smallest box, turn it base up, and place it to your left (the group's right).*

Well, sportsmen and women have to be very *determined* to compete in their sport. They will train hard, perhaps wiping their forehead with one of these.

*Bring out sweat bands and place them on top of the box.*

Have you ever seen gymnasts performing? They sometimes fall, but they bounce back up and keep going. They are determined to do their best.

Christians have to be determined as well. After all, they follow one of the most determined people ever—Jesus. He was determined to help people get to know God. Christians believe that, to do this, he had to die on a cross.

*Bring out the cross and place it on the box with the sweatbands.*

Christians also believe that he came back to life. They try to follow Jesus' determination to help others get to know God for themselves.

*Pause. Bring out the second box, turn it base up, and place it to your right, leaving a small gap between the two boxes.*

Sportspeople need to work in teams for games like football, hockey or rugby. Even solo sports, like tennis or running, need teams: Andy Murray or Usain Bolt will have people working with them, such as the coach, manager and physiotherapist. They *depend* on these other team members.

*Take the baton and place it on the box.*

Athletes running a relay race know how important it is to have a good team and to work well together, to depend on each other. If they drop the baton, they are disqualified and their race is over.

So it is with Christians. They depend on having a team around them, to encourage them, share stories with them and pray with them.

*Show picture or model of a church and place on the box.*

Their team is the church—and that doesn't mean the building. It means the people inside. They depend on each other.

*Pause. Bring out the third box, turn it base up and place it on top of the first and second boxes, forming a podium.*

I know that when you play sport, you play fair—you never foul anyone and never cheat.

*Take the whistle and place it on the box.*

But occasionally you may accidentally foul someone, so it's good to have a referee or umpire there to keep control and maintain *discipline*—someone who knows the rules.

Christians need discipline, too, and they go to their holy book for that.

*Show the Bible and place it on the third box.*

The Bible, with its stories and words full of God's love, gives them inspiration and helps them to know how they should live their lives.

*Pause.*

Determination... Dependence... Discipline... These are on three different steps at the moment, but they are all winners, all equally important in training and in living a faithful life. Have you noticed that after the medal ceremony, all three winning athletes join together on the top step?

*Bring all the props on to the top box.*

It's the same for Christians—except they believe that everyone can be a winner!

*

# Bibliography

Lilo Ljubisic, *The Challenge of Change*, audio download (from http://liloinspires.com, 2011)

Sally Magnusson, *The Flying Scotsman: A biography* (Quartet, 1981)

Jesse Owens with Paul Neimark, *Jesse: The Man Who Outran Hitler* (Ballantine Books, 1978)

*

**What Makes a Winner?** is also available as a Barnabas RE Day of storytelling, role-play, drama and games, exploring the connections between faith, belief, personal motivation and physical education.

# Barnabas RE Days

Barnabas RE Days can offer a full day's programme to your school to explore Christianity creatively with primary-aged children through storytelling, drama or music, according to the skills of the Barnabas in Schools team member.

## The Barnabas RE Day approach

We value the spiritual life of children, so we embrace an open-ended, exploratory approach when exploring Christian values and Bible stories through the creative arts. No assumptions are made about prior knowledge or expectations concerning personal belief; instead, children are encouraged to use the imagination to immerse themselves playfully in key faith stories to ask questions, suggest possible answers to dilemmas—and engage with Christian beliefs in a non-confrontational and frequently light-hearted way that supports RE, PSE and SMSC provision. Appropriate differentiation is made in style and content to allow for pupil age and ability, and support materials are also provided.

The sessions use different creative arts, according to the strengths of the Barnabas in Schools team member undertaking your booking, and include storytelling, music, mime or drama. The material is based on Bible stories, contemporary life illustrations and shared experience.

## Comments from recent Barnabas RE Days

*This was a most enjoyable day for our pupils and staff—very inspirational. Thank you.*
FINCHAMPSTEAD CE VA PRIMARY SCHOOL, NEAR WOKINGHAM

*Every member of staff felt that this course met its objective fully. Children were able to recall facts and had understood clearly.*
HUNTON CE PRIMARY SCHOOL, HUNTON, MAIDSTONE

For information on themes, costs, how to book and other FAQ, please go to:
www.barnabasinschools.org.uk/barnabas-re-days/

# Barnabas in Schools INSET

Barnabas in Schools INSET is designed to encourage and equip teachers for teaching Christianity with an RE Syllabus for Foundation, KS1 and KS2.

Training sessions include tried-and-tested ideas for collective worship, approaching the Bible creatively in RE lessons, and exploring ways of communication and understanding the Christian story through drama, music, story-telling and art.

An INSET session lasts two hours, with the option to run two sessions on one day.

To find out more, please go to www.barnabasinschools.org.uk/inset-and-professional-development/